THE ART OF SOCIAL MEDIA GROWTH FOR SMALL BUSINESSES

MASTERING THE DIGITAL WORLD - A BLUEPRINT FOR SMALL BUSINESS SUCCESS

Trina Brooks

TABLE OF CONTENT

CHAPTER ONE

Introduction: My Path from Zero to Six Figures in Social Media Success

Today's fast-paced, globally linked world has made social media an invaluable resource for small businesses looking to expand and succeed. The emergence of social media platforms such as Facebook, Instagram, Twitter, and LinkedIn has revolutionized the approaches by which businesses interact with their client base, advertise their goods and services, and establish their brand. I welcome you to take a journey through my personal experiences and insights in my book, "The Art of Social Media Growth for Small Businesses," which provides a thorough guide to navigating the ever-changing social media landscape for business success.

A Humble Beginning

As with other worthwhile endeavors, my entry into the realm of social media had its beginnings. I had a modest budget and a straightforward idea when I launched my little firm. Conventional marketing and advertising techniques were expensive and frequently produced ambiguous outcomes. At the start of the digital era, I noticed that social media could help businesses of all kinds compete on an even playing field. Social media provided an affordable means of expanding one's brand, interacting personally with potential clients, and reaching a larger audience.

The Social Media's Power

I was first introduced to social media's enormous potential for small businesses through my early interactions with it. I've seen firsthand how an engaging image or thoughtfully written post can grab readers' interest and start a conversation. Social media's real-time nature provided for quick response, which helped me to comprehend the needs, wants, and worries of my audience. This newfound agility gave me a competitive edge I had never had before, and it was transformational.

The Art of Connection

My knowledge of social media in the beginning was restricted to its surface features. But the more I explored the platforms, the more I realized that social media was more than just a broadcast medium for advertising. It served as a way to establish human connections with people. The revelation was a turning point in my path. I started putting more of an emphasis on fostering relationships than just gaining followers. I learned the true art of connection by being genuine in my interactions with my audience and providing value through educational and entertaining content.

Learning from Mistakes

My journey to social media success was not without its share of obstacles and disappointments. Along the journey, I faced many difficulties, such as poor content production, lost engagement opportunities, and sporadic negative feedback from disgruntled clients. But every disappointment turned into a priceless lesson that helped me understand the value of resiliency, flexibility, and the necessity of constantly improving my approach.

Navigating the Digital Landscape

Being aware of changes in the digital landscape and being flexible became essential. New platforms appeared, trends evolved, and algorithms changed. Maintaining awareness and being open to change were necessary for navigating this always changing landscape. To stay up to date with the latest developments in the sector, I looked for materials, went to workshops, and followed authorities. Changing with the times to fit the social media landscape became essential to my path.

Building a Community

Creating a community around my brand was one of the most fulfilling parts of my journey. Social media gave me the opportunity to meet people who were interested in my goods or services and who had similar interests. These relationships were about building loyalty and a sense of belonging, not just business. By interacting with my community, promoting conversations, and soliciting their opinions, I strengthened the bonds I had already established with them and enhanced my business.

Celebrating Successes

Numerous significant and insignificant turning points were encountered along the path to social media success. From the first post that went viral to the first customer who became a brand advocate, these moments of triumph served as fuel for my determination. What started off as a modestly funded initiative had grown into a flourishing business. My little firm started with nothing and has since expanded to generate six figures in sales. Celebrating these victories gave me inspiration to keep going and served as a reminder of the progress I had achieved.

The Ongoing Journey

The journey to social media success is not a one-time event but an ongoing process. I want to impart the knowledge, techniques, and lessons I've learned along the way in this book. "The Art of Social Media Growth for Small Businesses" is a thorough manual for small business owners who want to use social media as a growth accelerator, not just a summary of my experiences. I'll give you useful counsel, detailed instructions, and feasible ideas to enable you to take advantage of social media's entire potential for your company.

The Book's Promise.

The following pages will teach you how to set specific goals and objectives for your small business, pinpoint your target market, select the best social media channels, and create a compelling content plan. I'll also guide you in building a loyal community, growing your follower base, and effectively engaging with your audience. You'll get insights into adjusting to the always shifting social media landscape as well as the essential metrics and analytics tools to gauge your success.

I'll be stressing the value of genuine connections, prioritizing quality over quantity, and using social media to foster relationships rather than just advertise goods and services throughout the book. I'll also share the strategies I used to overcome common pitfalls and challenges that small businesses often face in the realm of social media.

By the end of this book, you'll be equipped with the knowledge and tools needed to embark on your own journey to social media success. You'll understand that it's not just about growth for the sake of growth; it's about growth with a purpose. The key is to master social media in order to engage with customers, grow your small business, and prosper in the digital era. I cordially encourage you to embark with me on this life-changing adventure, where the success of your small business is powered by the art of social media. If I could go from zero to six figures with the power of social media, so can you.

CHAPTER TWO

Setting the Stage for Success

In the ever-evolving landscape of social media, setting the stage for success is crucial for small businesses looking to harness its immense potential. This chapter, titled "Defining Your Small Business Goals: The Importance of Clear Objectives and Setting Specific, Measurable Goals," serves as the cornerstone of our journey through "The Art of Social Media Growth for Small Businesses."

The Significance of Setting Clear Goals

At the heart of any successful social media strategy lies a well-defined set of goals. These goals are more than mere aspirations; they are the foundation upon which your entire social media approach is built. For small businesses, the difference between aimlessly navigating the social media landscape and achieving meaningful growth often boils down to the clarity and specificity of their objectives.

From Ambition to Action

Early social media involvement is frequently characterized by zeal and aspiration. But in the absence of a defined plan, these feelings on their own could be ambiguous and insufficient. When it comes to social media, small business owners frequently have similar goals in mind, including "growing brand awareness" or "acquiring more clients." Although these aspirations are valuable, in order to create a conducive environment for success, they need to be turned into concrete objectives.

The Journey Begins with the Destination

Envision setting out on a cross-country road trip with no specific destination in sight. It's possible to drive erratically, never sure if you're approaching your destination. Setting clear social media goals is like deciding on a destination for your journey. It offers guidance on how to get where you want to go as well as a sense of purpose.

The Importance of Clear Objectives

An effective social media strategy needs well-defined objectives to be successful. They act as the cornerstone for each and every post, interaction, and piece of content you produce. This is why they are necessary:

1. Alignment: Having specific goals can help your social media initiatives complement your broader business objectives. They make sure that every move you make on social media advances the expansion and prosperity of your business.

2. Measurability: Having well-defined goals gives you a benchmark to gauge your success against. This measurable quality is essential to figuring out what's working and what needs to be improved.

3. Focus: It's simple to become distracted by trends, unrelated facts, and distractions in the busy world of social media. Well-defined goals aid in maintaining concentration on the essential aspects of your company.

4. Accountability: With defined objectives, you can hold yourself and your team accountable for achieving specific outcomes. Action and outcomes are fueled by this accountability.

Setting Specific, Measurable Goals

While it is obvious that creating goals is important, how you define them matters greatly. Ambiguous, non-specific objectives can cause confusion and annoyance. Setting **SMART** (specific, measurable, attainable, relevant, and time-bound) goals is crucial to genuinely laying the groundwork for success.

Specific Objectives

The foundation of a successful goal-setting strategy is specificity. A more targeted goal may be, "I aim to increase my Instagram followers by 20% over the next three months," as opposed to just stating, "I want more followers." Specificity eliminates room for interpretation while offering guidance and clarity.

Measurable Goals

Objectives: Measurability is important because it lets you monitor your development and assess your level of success. You can respond to queries like "Did we achieve what we set out to do?" with measurable goals. In order to build on the previous illustration, you can determine whether you've achieved your 20% goal by tracking the growth of your Instagram followers.

Achievable Goals

Dream big, but don't forget to set realistic objectives. Unattainable goals can cause dissatisfaction and disappointment. Achievable objectives combine ambition and practicality in a harmonious manner.Think about the following: "Can I achieve this goal with the time, money, and experience I have available?"

Relevant Goals

Relevance ensures that your social media goals are aligned with your broader business objectives. Your objectives must directly support the expansion of your business, the building of your brand, or the engagement of your clients. If a goal fails to do this, reevaluate its applicability.

Time-Bound Goals

Time-bound goals have a set deadline. A time-bound goal would be, "I aim to increase my Instagram followers by 20% within the next three months," as opposed to, "I want to increase my Instagram followers." Setting deadlines makes you feel pressed for time and keeps you on course.

Applying SMART Goals to Your Small Business

Let's use a small business example to demonstrate the effectiveness of SMART goals:

Objective: Boost website visitors using social media.

SMART Goal: During the next six months, increase website traffic by 15% by utilizing a mix of engagement, content sharing, and targeted social media advertising on sites like Facebook and Instagram.

Specific: The objective is clear about boosting website traffic using social media channels and identifies the platforms that should be prioritized.

Measurable: A clear indicator of success is the 15% increase in website traffic.

Achievable: Content sharing, interaction, and targeted advertising are all taken into account as ways to accomplish the goal.

Relevant: Increasing website traffic aligns with the broader business objective of expanding the online presence and, potentially, generating more leads or sales.

Time-Bound: A period of six months creates a sense of accountability and urgency.

With this SMART goal, you have a specific plan of action and an achievable objective rather than just wishing for greater website visitors.

Your Journey to Success

Your social media success story begins with precisely and clearly defining your small business goals. When created with the SMART framework, these objectives will operate as your North Star, directing your activities, tracking your advancement, and preserving your alignment with your overall business objectives.

In the chapters to come, we'll delve deeper into how to transform these goals into actionable strategies, identify the right social media platforms to achieve them, and create engaging content that resonates with your audience. As we proceed through "The Art of Social Media Growth for Small Businesses," you will discover useful information, detailed instructions, and practical guidance to help you realize the greatest possible return on investment from social media for your business. Your goals are the first step on the path to success, and as we work together to negotiate the ever-changing social media landscape, your journey will soon take on even more excitement and meaning.

Identifying Your Target Audience:

One cannot emphasize how crucial it is for small businesses to identify and comprehend their target audience when on the path to social media success. This section, "Identifying Your Target Audience: Understanding Your Ideal Customer, Building Customer Personas for Precision," is a critical piece of the puzzle within "The Art of Social Media Growth for Small Businesses."

The Power of Knowing Your Audience

Social media is a dynamic and constantly evolving platform that helps businesses engage with their target market. However, how well you understand your target will determine how successful your efforts are. The goal should be to build real relationships with people who are truly interested in what your company has to offer, not to gain as many followers as possible.

Why Your Ideal Customer Matters

1. Tailored Content: Knowing your ideal customer allows you to create content that resonates with their needs, preferences, and pain points. This customization fosters trust and increases engagement.

2. Effective Marketing: Quantity is not as important as quality. Knowing who your ideal client is will help you focus your efforts more effectively, cut down on waste, and increase profits.

3. Product Development: Gaining a thorough grasp of your target market can help you create new products, enhance existing ones, or even come up with creative ways to meet their needs.

4. Competitive Advantage: You stand out from rivals that adopt a one-size-fits-all strategy when you establish a personal connection with your audience.

Understanding Your Ideal Customer

Prior to delving into the actualities of creating customer profiles, let's talk about the idea of the perfect client, sometimes known as the "buyer persona." Your ideal client isn't just a general population; rather, it's a specific sample of people who are most likely to interact with your business over time.

Defining Your Ideal Customer

Begin by posing the following queries:

➢ Whom is your business aimed at serving? What are the characteristics of the people who would benefit most from your products or services?

➢ What are their goals and challenges? What drives them, and what challenges do they encounter?

➢ Where do they go online to pass the time? Which social media platforms, forums, or online communities do they frequent?

> What issues can your business help them with? How does your product or service provide a solution to their pain points?

> Why should they choose you? What unique selling point makes your company the best option for this client?

Building Customer Personas for Precision

It's time to develop customer personas for accuracy now that you have a clear understanding of your ideal client. Detailed, semi-fictional depictions of your ideal clients are called customer personas. They assist you in developing a deeper understanding, empathy, and visualization of your audience.

Creating Customer Personas

Typical components of customer personas include the following:

Demographics: This includes age, gender, income, location, and other essential data points that describe your ideal customer's background.

Challenges and Goals: What are their professional or personal objectives, and what impediments are they facing? Knowing this enables you to customize your solutions and content.

Needs and Pain Points: What needs, anxieties, or difficulties are they now facing? How can your business properly handle these?

Where do they spend their online time? What is their behavior and preference? Which kind of information appeals to them? Do they use particular social media sites more frequently?

Consumption of Media and Content: How do people take in information? Do they watch videos, listen to podcasts, or read a lot of books?

Buying Habits: What criteria do people use to decide what to buy? What elements play a role in their decisions?

Values and Beliefs: How can your business be in line with their basic values and beliefs?

An Example of a Customer Persona

Let's bring the concept of a customer persona to life with an example:

- ➢ Name of Persona: Sarah
- ➢ Demographics:
- ➢ Age: 32
- ➢ Gender: Female
- ➢ Location: New York City's urban professional district

Objectives and Obstacles:

Sarah wants to emphasize self-care and live a healthy lifestyle.

Difficulties: Time constraints brought on by a demanding profession and a bustling city life.

Requirements and Problems:

Need: She's searching for easy, nutritious dinner ideas.

Problems: Not enough time for organizing and preparing meals.

Behavior and Preferences:

Active on Pinterest and Instagram to get cooking inspiration.

Prefers meals that are easy to follow, quick, and fit into her hectic schedule.

Media and Content Consumption:

➢ Enjoys watching quick cooking videos and reading lifestyle websites.
➢ Listens to podcasts on her way to work every day.
➢ Buying Habits.

- Does internet research on things before buying them.
- Values organic and sustainable options.
- Values and Beliefs:
- Supports local businesses and sustainable practices.

Sarah, the customer persona, provides a thorough grasp of a person who fits the needs and beliefs of your business. Developing marketing plans and content specifically for individuals such as Sarah will greatly increase your influence and interaction on social media.

The Role of Customer Personas in Social Media Success

Customer personas are dynamic, changing along with your audience and business. Your product development, engagement initiatives, social media advertising, and content creation are all guided by these personalities. They are essential for communicating with your audience directly and in a way that speaks to their needs and wants.

We will go into how to use your knowledge of your target market and customer profiles in the subsequent sections of this book to help you choose the best social media platforms, create engaging content, cultivate an engaged community, and track your progress. You'll see how exact audience targeting can make all the difference in the world when it comes to your small business succeeding on social media with each step.

As you negotiate the ever-changing social media landscape, your most precious assets will be your ideal client and the consumer profiles you develop. You'll discover how to put this information into practice along our joint journey, creating a devoted and involved audience that propels your small business to new heights.

Navigating the Big Four: Facebook, Twitter, Instagram, and LinkedIn

Small businesses are frequently faced with a difficult choice in the constantly changing social media landscape:

which platforms should they devote their time and resources to in order to effectively reach their audience?"

Choosing the social media channels that will best support your business's growth is similar to picking the best soil. Selecting the appropriate platform is essential for success as each one has its own user base, features, and engagement opportunities. In order to fully understand the "Big Four," let's first examine the importance of platform selection:

Tailored Reach: A range of audiences are drawn to different platforms. The first step to making sure your message reaches your ideal clients successfully is figuring out where they spend their time.

Resource optimization: Time and resources are frequently scarce for small businesses. Your return on investment is maximized when you concentrate your efforts on platforms that support your objectives.

Brand Consistency: In branding, consistency is essential. Focusing on a small number of channels enables you to keep your brand's message and image consistent throughout the digital space.

Possibilities for Engagement: Every platform provides a variety of ways to interact with your audience. Selecting platforms that complement your content and manner of engagement is crucial to developing an engaged community.

A Deep Dive into Platform Selection

Let's now examine the distinctive qualities of the "Big Four" social media networks: LinkedIn, Instagram, Twitter, **Facebook, and Instagram.** These platforms all have unique benefits and target different audiences and types of content.

1. Facebook Audience: Facebook is the biggest social media network in the world, with over 2.8 billion monthly active members. It can be used to reach a variety of audiences because it appeals to a broad population.

Content types: Text, photos, videos, and live streaming are just a few of the types that Facebook supports.

Possibilities for Engagement: It's a great forum for creating a community and encouraging dialogue. In particular, Facebook Groups facilitate deeper friendships.

Advertising: Facebook has strong advertising capabilities with a variety of ad styles and accurate audience targeting.

2. Twitter Audience: With a focus on real-time communication, Twitter boasts 330 million monthly active users. It draws a wide range of people, including businesses and individuals.

Content Formats: Twitter is well-known for its brief messages, or tweets, which make it appropriate for exchanging news and updates as well as having discussions.

Possibilities for Engagement: It serves as a forum for current dialogue and interaction. You can reach a wider audience with your content by using hashtags.

Twitter offers advertising alternatives that help you reach a wider audience and interact with more targeted audiences.

3. Instagram

Audience: Instagram boasts over 1 billion monthly active users, with a strong focus on visual content. It's especially well-liked among younger audiences.

Content Formats: Instagram is dominated by visual content, such as pictures and quick videos. IGTV, Reels, and Stories provide even more chances for interaction.

Possibilities for Engagement: It's the perfect medium for aesthetically presenting goods, services, and brand elements. Instagram uses direct messages, comments, and likes to encourage interaction.

Advertising: Precise audience targeting and aesthetically pleasing ad forms are possible with Instagram advertising, which is frequently combined with Facebook ads.

4. LinkedIn

Audience: LinkedIn's user base is focused on business and professionalism. With more than 774 million members, it's a useful B2B and professional networking tool.

Content Formats: Professional material, such as job listings, articles, and company updates, are the main focus of LinkedIn.

Engagement Opportunities: This is a great place to network professionally, exchange industry insights, and become an authority in your field.

Advertising: To reach professionals and decision-makers, LinkedIn provides a variety of B2B advertising solutions, such as sponsored content and InMail.

Choosing the Right Platforms for Your Business

Your target audience and business objectives should be taken into consideration while selecting social media sites. Take into account the following elements to choose the ideal combination:

1. Business Objectives: What particular goals do you have for social media? Is the objective lead generation, customer involvement, brand exposure, or something else?

2. Target Market: Who is the perfect client for you? Take into account behavior, hobbies, and demography. Your decisions should be based on the platforms that your audience uses most often.

3. Content Type: What kind of Content is best produced by your company? Which types of content do you prefer to read, watch, or receive brief updates?

4. Resources: Examine your time, staff, and financial resources to see what you have available, then select platforms that work for you.

5. Competitive Landscape: Examine the areas in which your rivals are present. It gives you some idea of where your target audience might be, even if you don't have to follow their example.

6. Analytics and Testing: Monitor performance on selected platforms on a regular basis and be ready to modify your plan in response to data and audience input.

Platform Selection in Practice

In order to illustrate how to select appropriate platforms for various business circumstances, let's look at two examples:

Scenario 1: An Artisan Bakery

Business Goals: Promote distinctive baked goods and raise brand awareness.

The intended audience comprises of aspiring caterers and culinary enthusiasts in the area.

Type of content: Visual material featuring delicious baked products.

Instagram was chosen as the platform because of its eye-catching aesthetic and chances for local engagement. Facebook to foster a more extensive local community.

Scenario 2: A B2B SaaS Startup

Business Goals: Generate leads, establish thought leadership.

Decision-makers, software engineers, and business experts are the target audience.

Content Type: Industry insights and in-depth publications.

LinkedIn is the preferred platform due to its extensive professional user base and potential for thought leadership. Twitter for interaction and real-time industry updates.

The platform choice in each case is in line with the target audience, content strengths, and specific goals of the company.

Adapting and Expanding Your Strategy

While choosing the appropriate platforms is an essential first step, it's also necessary to maintain flexibility. Social media platforms can fluctuate in popularity and efficacy due to their dynamic nature. Monitor audience interaction, evaluate the effectiveness of the platforms you've selected on a regular basis, and be ready to adjust your approach as needed.

As you proceed with "The Art of Social Media Growth for Small Businesses," you'll learn how to produce interesting content, increase the number of people who follow you, and gauge your progress on the selected platforms. You'll be well-positioned to maximize your social media presence and propel growth and success for your small business if you choose your platforms wisely and have a thorough understanding of your target demographic.

CHAPTER THREE

Crafting an Engaging Content Strategy:

Developing a compelling content strategy is essential to drawing in viewers and building deep relationships in the ever-changing world of social media.

Developing a Content Strategy

Your content strategy is the cornerstone that directs your social media endeavors. It describes the things, times, and methods of your audience communication. You can make sure that every piece of content you produce advances the main objectives of your business by creating a strong content strategy.

The Building Blocks of a Content Strategy

Goals and Objectives: Your content strategy starts with well-defined objectives. Are you trying to raise sales, create leads, enhance website traffic, or raise brand awareness? Your entire strategy is shaped by your aims.

Target Audience: Knowing your audience is pivotal. Your content should resonate with their preferences, interests, and pain points. Adapt your content to meet their particular requirements.

Content Type: Choose a format for your content that complements your audience and brand. Blog entries, films, infographics, podcasts, and/or a mix of these could be included in this.

Content Topics: List the topics and themes that will be covered in your content. These subjects must to be pertinent to your target market, industry, and corporate objectives.

Content Calendar: Schedule the times and frequency of your publishing by creating a content calendar. To keep people interested, you must remain consistent.

Keyword and SEO Strategy: To make sure your target audience can find your material, use keyword research and SEO best practices, if relevant.

Content Promotion: Consider how you'll promote your content. Email marketing, social media advertising, and influencer collaborations are a few examples of this.

Performance Measurement: To monitor the effectiveness of your content, set up key performance indicators (KPIs). Metrics like website visits, conversion rates, and engagement rates may be part of this.

The Core Elements of a Content Strategy

Let's take a closer look at the fundamental components of a content strategy:

1. Goals and Objectives

Knowing exactly what you want to accomplish should be the first step in developing your content strategy. Small businesses often aim to achieve the following on social media:

- ➢ Increasing brand awareness
- ➢ Growing your follower base
- ➢ Generating leads or sales
- ➢ Fostering a relationship with customers
- ➢ Developing an intellectual leadership

These goals should be matched with specific objectives. One goal that might be associated with "increasing brand awareness" is "gaining 500 new followers per month."

2. Target Audience

The foundation of any successful content strategy is an understanding of your audience. Their wants, needs, and pain areas should all be directly addressed in your content. Consider:

- ➢ Demographics: Age, gender, location, occupation, etc.
- ➢ Interests and hobbies
- ➢ Behavior: How do they use social media?
- ➢ Challenges and pain points

> Create detailed customer personas to ensure your content resonates with your audience.

3. Content Type

The type of content you produce should align with your brand and your audience's preferences. Among the typical content kinds are:

> Blog posts
> Videos Infographics
> Podcasts
> Webinars Posts on social media

Your content type should cater to your audience's preferred way of consuming information.

4. Content Topics

Content topics should revolve around your industry, your brand values, and your audience's interests. If you want to find pertinent subjects that are also probably going to rank well in search engines, think about doing keyword research.

5. Content Calendar

A content calendar helps you plan when and how often you'll publish content. It guarantees consistency, which is essential to sustaining interest. When making a content calendar, take into account the following factors:

> ➤ Frequency of posting
> ➤ Optimal posting times
> ➤ Seasonal or timely content

6. Keyword and SEO Strategy

If your content is published online, consider incorporating keyword research and SEO best practices to improve its discoverability. Make use of pertinent keywords in your meta descriptions and content, and optimize your photos to load more quickly.

7. Content Promotion

Just as crucial as producing content is promoting it. Consider the strategy you'll use to expose your audience to your material. Potential tactics could be:

- ➤ Email marketing
- ➤ Social media advertising
- ➤ Influencer partnerships
- ➤ Sharing in online forums or communities

8. Performance Measurement

Establish key performance indicators (KPIs) to gauge your content's effectiveness. Among your KPIs could be:

- ➤ Engagement rates: Likes, comments, shares
- ➤ Website visits from social media
- ➤ Turnover percentages: enrollments, purchases, etc.
- ➤ Click-through rates (CTR) for links

Regularly assess your content's performance and adjust your strategy based on the data.

Planning and consistency are crucial elements of an effective content strategy. This is why they are important:

1. Audience Expectations

Consistency aids in establishing audience expectations. Your audience is more likely to interact with your content when they are aware of when new content is released.

2. Brand Image

A strong brand image is developed via consistency in tone, style, and quality. It promotes acknowledgment and trust.

3. Time Management

Make a plan in advance to avoid last-minute stress and to save time when creating content. It makes room for more deliberate and well-planned content.

4. Flexibility

While preparation is essential, flexibility is just as crucial. Be willing to modify your content strategy in response to input from the audience, market developments, and performance data.

Adapting to Your Business

A content strategy's fundamental components provide a guide for your social media endeavors. But, it's crucial to modify these components to fit your specific business and target market. One business's model might not be suitable for another's needs. Evaluate the effectiveness of your content strategy on a regular basis and be ready to make changes as necessary.

In the sessions that follow in "The Art of Social Media Growth for Small Businesses," you'll explore the nuances of crafting compelling content, growing your follower base, and measuring your success. In the dynamic world of social media, a well-defined content strategy will put you in a good position to engage your audience and propel small business growth.

The Art of Storytelling on Social Media

The art of storytelling has become a potent tool for small businesses looking to establish a deeper connection with their audience in the ever-changing landscape of social media. An essential part of "The Art of Social Media Growth for Small Businesses" is this chapter, "The Art of Storytelling on Social Media: Telling Your Brand Story, Creating a Connection with Your Audience."

The Power of Storytelling

Storytelling is an ancient custom that serves as a basic means of human connection, communication, and world-making. Storytelling has a special place in the social media world. It's a smart way to interact, inform, and establish a bond with your audience rather than just a way to pass the time.

Telling Your Brand Story

A story behind your brand. It has a mission, a goal, and a history. You may effectively communicate the essence of your business and establish a personal connection with your audience by sharing your brand story on social media. Here's how to properly create and communicate your brand story:

Origin Story: Let's start with how your company got its start. Explain the "why" that led to its formation. What was the intended solution? Who were the main figures in its infancy?

Values and Mission: Clearly state the goals and values of your company. Describe the significance of these principles and how you act and make decisions based on them.

Impact on Customers: Share success stories about how your good or service has helped customers. Provide references, case studies, or experiences that highlight your worth.

Behind-the-Scenes: Describe the behind-the-scenes activities for your audience. Explain the daily activities, present your team, and demonstrate the commitment to your work.

Obstacles and Achievements: Honestly discuss the difficulties your company has encountered. Tell stories of resiliency, flexibility, and life lessons gained.

Future Vision: Share with others what you see as the future. What direction is your business taking, and how will it keep making an impact?

Creating a Connection with Your Audience

The art of storytelling involves more than just narrating your own story; it also involves creating a connection with the experiences, feelings, and stories of your audience. Take into account the following techniques to engage your audience through storytelling:

Relatability: Write stories that connect to the experiences of your readers. Talk about the shared struggles, goals, and feelings of your audience.

Empathy: Express empathy by recognizing the difficulties or applauding the accomplishments of your listeners. Tell them stories that show you are aware of and concerned about their needs.

User-Generated Content: Invite clients to submit their own testimonials about your goods or services. Repost and honor user-generated content to demonstrate your brand's impact in the real world.

Interactive Storytelling: Produce engaging interactive material that lets people connects with your brand's narrative. Utilize surveys, tests, or Q&A sessions, for instance, to engage your audience.

Maintaining a connection requires consistency, which is essential. Share stories that embody your brand's mission and values on a regular basis. This constancy fosters confidence.

Story Arcs: To organize your information, use storytelling techniques such as story arcs. Introduce the problem or issue, offer a workaround, and end with a resolution that your audience can relate to.

Elements of Compelling Social Media Stories

It's crucial to comprehend the following crucial components of an engaging story in order to write captivating stories for social media:

1. A Relatable Protagonist

Either your brand or a customer's experience ought to take center stage. Their experiences and feelings should be relatable to the audience.

2. Conflict or Challenge

A primary conflict or problem is often at the center of an engaging story. This could be a social issue, a personal challenge, or a problem that your product or service helps to solve.

3. Resolution

Stories ought to provide a conclusion or a way out of the problem. Demonstrate how your company's name, goods, or services help people succeed or overcome obstacles.

4. Emotion

Emotions are the driving force behind storytelling. To emotionally engage your audience, use vivid language, eye-catching imagery, and personal experiences.

5. Authenticity

Sincerity is essential. Tell sincere stories and express sincere feelings. Content that is too planned or polished should be avoided since it may come out as unauthentic.

6. Visual Appeal

Images and videos are examples of visual content that improves social media storytelling. It successfully catches the eye and expresses feelings.

Incorporating Storytelling into Your Social Media Strategy

There are several ways to incorporate storytelling into your social media plan. The following actions can help you include storytelling in your content strategy:

1. Visual Storytelling

Make the most of pictures and videos to visually express your story. Share brief yet powerful stories on social media sites such as TikTok, Pinterest, and Instagram.

2. Live Content

To engage with your audience in real time, think about utilizing the live streaming capabilities available on websites like Facebook, Instagram, and YouTube. Storytelling during live sessions can be spontaneous and uncensored.

3. Regular Story Series

Create regular story series or segments. A "Meet the Team" series, for instance, could present various team members and their responsibilities inside your business's structure.

4. Customer Spotlights

Emphasize the experiences of your clients. Post user-generated content, success stories, or testimonials from them that demonstrate how your product or service has improved their lives.

5. Interactive Content

Engage your audience with interactive content that invites them to participate in your story. Contests, assessments, and polls can develop an interactive story.

6. Challenges and Hashtags

Make original challenges and hashtags that are relevant to your brand's story. To build a feeling of community, invite your audience to use these hashtags to share their experiences.

A Case Examination: "The Little Startup That Sparked Social Media Success"

In a digital corner of the business world, there stood a small startup named "GrowthSpark Solutions." On the surface, it was just another small venture in the vast sea of businesses.

But behind the screens, there was a story waiting to be told – my story.

As the founder of "GrowthSpark Solutions," I had a dream. It was about more than just providing services; it was about building a vibrant center for the expansion of social media, helping small businesses, and establishing relationships with business owners. "GrowthSpark Solutions" was founded with my love for digital marketing and my goal of becoming the go-to source for small business owners.

Telling Your Brand Story.

My brand story was one of determination and growth. My journey included:

Origin Story: How "GrowthSpark Solutions" started as a one-person operation, overcame the difficulties of being unprepared, and developed into a vibrant group of people committed to helping small businesses.

Values and Mission: My steadfast dedication to supplying social media solutions that are both economical and successful, aiding companies in making a lasting impression on the internet, and furnishing tools for business owners.

Customer Impact: Testimonials of entrepreneurs who obtained insightful information from our tools, as well as success tales of small business owners who saw a transformation in their social media presence.

Challenges and Triumphs: There were several challenges along the way, such as the dynamic social media algorithms and the intense rivalry in the digital marketing industry. However, every obstacle turned into a chance for creativity and enlightenment.

Future Vision: In my vision, "GrowthSpark Solutions" would develop further, providing new services, partnerships, and tools to help small businesses succeed on social media.

Creating a Connection with Your Audience.

"GrowthSpark Solutions" wasn't just a startup; it became a place where social media dreams thrived. My storytelling strategy included:

User-Generated Content: After utilizing our services and resources, I urged small company owners to submit their success stories. Clients discussed how our solutions helped them expand on social media and their experiences using them.

Interactive Storytelling: I started "Success Spotlight" events, where business owners would tell their stories and our audience would inquire and learn.

Visual Storytelling: "GrowthSpark Solutions" disseminated images of cheerful business owners, growth figures, and the transforming potential of social media success via social media channels.

Consistency: Throughout its narrative, the startup never wavered in its dedication to helping entrepreneurs and small enterprises. It was more than simply a business; it sparked the expansion of social media.

As I shared my brand story, a loyal community formed around "GrowthSpark Solutions." Owners of small businesses and entrepreneurs felt that they were part of a movement that celebrated the success, expansion, and support of social media, rather than merely a provider of services.

One day, a small business owner named Lisa discovered "GrowthSpark Solutions." She came across a testimonial from a different business owner who had used our services and had noticed a noticeable increase in their social media visibility. Lisa decided to get in touch as her business was having trouble taking off on social media.

With the help of our knowledgeable staff and the "GrowthSpark Solutions" community, Lisa's business completely changed its social media profile. Our startup was essential to her journey towards realizing her aim of growing her business and reaching a wider audience.

Lisa's story, intertwined with mine, became a testament to the power of storytelling and the profound impact a small startup can have when it weaves its brand story into the lives of its customers.

The popularity of "GrowthSpark Solutions" served as evidence of the skill of social media storytelling. My humble venture became a location where social media aspirations came true and growth was welcomed and encouraged by sharing my story, accepting a greater purpose, and raising a vibrant community of small business owners and entrepreneurs.

Visual Content Mastery

The value of visual content is immeasurable in a time when our attention spans are getting shorter and there is a steady stream of information vying for our attention.

The Power of Images and Videos

The foundation of efficient social media communication is now visual material. It can fascinate, engage, and quickly express complicated messages since it transcends the confines of language. Here's why photos and videos are important:

1. Visual Appeal

Text is not as efficiently processed by human brains as visual information is. Videos and pictures with good composition are more likely to grab viewers' attention.

2. Emotional Impact

Images have a special power to arouse feelings. Visuals evoke strong emotions in viewers, whether it's through the happiness seen in a customer testimonial film or the motivational message presented in an infographic.

3. Information in a Snap

A succinct film or a well-designed infographic can clarify a point that might require several paragraphs of text. This conciseness is a useful quality in an era of excessive information.

4. Shareability

The likelihood of visual content being shared on social media is higher. Your brand's visibility rises and your reach is expanded when your audience shares your content.

5. Brand Recognition

Brand awareness is aided by consistency in visual branding aspects including color schemes, fonts, and style. Your material should instantly become associated with your brand when it is viewed by your audience.

Design Tips and Tools

Mastering visual content doesn't require a degree in graphic design. Even tiny businesses can produce eye-catching pictures that captivate their audience with the correct advice and resources.

1. Know Your Audience

When creating visual content, the first step is to understand your target audience. Take into account their hobbies, annoyances, and preferences. Make your images seem more real to them.

2. Consistent Branding

Keep your logo constant throughout all of your images. To make sure that your readers can quickly identify the content as being yours, stick to the same style, fonts, and color scheme.

3. Keep It Simple

Most powerful graphics are frequently those that are kept simple. Steer clear of intricate and cluttered designs. Communicate your point simply.

4. Storytelling through Visuals

Use videos and pictures to tell a story. Demonstrate the process, the journey, and the change. Using stories to tell your brand's story makes it appealing to your target audience.

5. High-Quality Images and Videos

Spend money on quality. Use videos and photos with high resolution to give it a polished appearance. Visuals of poor quality can turn off viewers.

6. Use of Text

Make the text readable if it's included in your graphic material. For clarity, make sure the text contrasts with the background and use readable fonts.

7. Understand Platform Specifications

The image and video parameters vary throughout social media networks. Make sure the content you're using is appropriate for the platform you're on.

8. User-Generated Content

Inspire the people in your audience to produce brand-related content. Repost content created by users to foster community and trust.

9. Visual Hierarchy

Guide your audience's eyes through your visual content. To highlight important components, apply the principles of visual hierarchy.

10. A/B Testing

Try out various visuals to determine which ones your audience responds to the most. You may improve your visual content strategy by using A/B testing.

Design Tools and Resources

Producing eye-catching content doesn't have to be difficult. The following materials and design tools can help you become an expert in visual content:

1. Canva

Canva is an online graphic design tool that is easy to use and provides templates, fonts, photos, and other design elements. It's perfect for making posters, social media graphics, and other things.

2. Adobe Spark

Another web-based design tool that makes the process simpler is Adobe Spark. It offers tools and templates for making images, web pages, and quick films.

3. Pexels and Unsplash

You can use royalty-free, high-quality photographs from these websites in your visual material. These are great places to look for eye-catching images.

4. Adobe Creative Cloud

Adobe Creative Cloud provides Photoshop and Illustrator as part of a professional design software suite for anyone looking for more sophisticated design skills.

5. Video Editing Tools

You can edit and make interesting films for social media with programs like Adobe Premiere Pro, Final Cut Pro, and even free ones like DaVinci Resolve.

6. Infographic Makers

Infographic production is made easier by programs like Venngage and Piktochart, which also help to make difficult material easier to understand.

7. Image Optimization Tools

You may compress images to make them load more quickly on websites and social media by using programs like TinyPNG or ImageOptim.

8. Social Media Schedulers

You can plan and organize your visual material with tools like Buffer and Hootsuite, which can help you maintain a constant online presence.

9. Platforms for user-generated content

You may gather and organize user-generated content to highlight the influence of your business with the aid of apps like Yotpo and TINT.

10. Educational Resources

You can learn the fundamentals of design and how to utilize design tools by watching online lessons and courses on sites like Udemy or YouTube.

Case Investigation: "The Visual Transformation of 'BloomCraft Decor'"

To illustrate the power of visual content mastery, let's dive into the story of "BloomCraft Decor," a small business that specializes in handcrafted home decor items.

Before embracing the skill of mastering visual content, "BloomCraft Decor" encountered a typical difficulty faced by small businesses: trying to make a name for themselves in the cutthroat e-commerce industry. Their internet presence lacked the same charm as their excellent items.

Despite having little money, the company owner chose to use graphic content to its fullest. They put the following tactics into practice:

High-Quality Product Images: "BloomCraft Decor" invested in professional product photography. Clear, finely detailed photos emphasized the beauty and skill of their products.

Consistent Branding: They selected a color palette and aesthetic that complemented the handmade, rustic feel of their brand. Every picture and video evoked the feeling of being in a warm, artisanal workshop.

Storytelling through Videos: Brief video snippets showed the steps involved in making each piece, from the acquisition of raw materials to the final product. These "artisan spotlight" videos demonstrated the attention to detail and humanized the brand.

User-Generated Content: The Company invited clients to upload pictures of their "BloomCraft Decor" accents in residences. These real, user-generated photos ended up being a great asset for the company.

Educational Infographics: To engage their audience further, "BloomCraft Decor" created infographics that explained the craftsmanship behind their products and offered tips for home decor.

The results were astounding. Engagement on social media and the brand's website grew dramatically as a result of the updated visual content approach. Customer testimonials—all of which featured user-generated images—rose significantly. "BloomCraft Decor" had a devoted following of people who conversed about current trends in home decor and excitedly awaited the arrival of new products.

"BloomCraft Decor's" transition from a faltering small business to a thriving brand was fueled primarily by visual material. Their story demonstrates the potential of mastering visual content, especially for low-resource businesses.

Visual Content Mastery as a Growth Strategy

Understanding visual content is a growth strategy that cuts across industry and size in the dynamic world of social media. Effective use of captivating images can be your secret weapon for increasing engagement, presenting a story, and eventually spurring growth, regardless of the size of your local business or small internet store. You'll discover how visual content mastery fits into your overall social media strategy as you proceed through "The Art of Social Media Growth for Small Businesses," from developing compelling ads to telling compelling stories and tracking your progress. In the always-changing world of social media, you can captivate your audience and take your small business to new heights by perfecting the art of visual content.

CHAPTER FOUR

Building a Loyal Community

Growing Your Follower Base

In the world of social media, having a large number of followers is frequently seen as a sign of success. However, it's not just about the quantity; it's about the quality and engagement of your followers. A key part of "The Art of Social Media Growth for Small Businesses" is this chapter, "Growing Your Follower Base: Strategies for Organic Growth, Engaging with Your Followers."

Strategies for Organic Growth

Although there are some quick fixes, such as purchasing followers or participating in follow-for-follow programs, these strategies hardly ever result in real, active followers. Conversely, organic growth concentrates on drawing in followers who are sincere in their interest in your content and brand. The following are tactics for natural growth:

1. Content Quality is King

The caliber of your content is the cornerstone of organic development. It must be worthwhile, pertinent, and interesting to your intended audience. Users are encouraged to follow and remain engaged by high-quality content.

2. Consistency Matters

Posting consistently is essential. A consistent publication schedule keeps readers interested and informed. Make plans and stick to a schedule by using social media scheduling tools.

3. Hashtags for Visibility

Using hashtags is crucial for finding content. Incorporate popular and pertinent hashtags into your content to expand your readership. But try not to use them excessively as that can come out as spam.

4. Collaborations and Cross-Promotion

Work together with influencers or other businesses in your niche. Through cross-promotion, a new audience that is perhaps interested in your content is introduced to your brand.

5. Engage with User-Generated Content Encourage your followers to create and share content related to your brand. Repost and honor user-generated material to foster a sense of community and trust.

6. Run Contests and Giveaways

Giveaways and contests are excellent ways to draw attention. To be eligible to win, participants should be required to like, follow, and share your content.

7. Engage with Trending Topics

Stay updated on trending topics and current events within your niche. To keep your content visible and relevant, interact with these topics.

8. Optimize Your Profile

A captivating bio, contact details, and an eye-catching profile image are essential components of an optimal social network page. Users are encouraged to follow you by these components.

9. Educational and Informative Content

Sharing enlightening or educational stuff demonstrates your worth and competence. You can draw and keep readers who are interested in learning from you with this kind of information.

10. Leverage Analytics

Keep an eye on your social media statistics to see what is and is not working. Make use of this information to enhance your approach and content.

Engaging with Your Followers

Having a large following is insufficient; you also need to actively interact with them. Engagement fosters loyalty and a sense of community. Here's how to interact with your followers effectively:

1. Respond to Comments and Messages

React quickly to direct messages and remarks. To create a feeling of connection, have meaningful interactions with your audience.

2. Ask Questions and Seek Feedback

By posing queries or requesting comments, you can promote involvement. This increases communication and yields insightful information.

3. Run Polls and Surveys

Surveys and polls are great tools for fostering engagement. They provide your followers with a sense of being heard and included in the choices you make.

4. Use Stories and Live Streams

Real-time engagement techniques include live streaming and stories. They offer a chance to establish a more intimate connection with your audience.

5. Share User-Generated Content

Sharing user-generated material is a great method to interact with your audience, as was previously discussed. It expresses gratitude and promotes the creation of more user-generated content.

6. Celebrate Milestones

Celebrate and acknowledge accomplishments, such as hitting a follower target, an anniversary, or the launch of a new product. The success of your followers is also your success.

7. Host Contests and Challenges

Contests and challenges aren't just for attracting new followers; they also keep your existing followers engaged and excited about your brand.

8. Highlight Customer Stories

Tell success stories about pleased clients and their use of your good or service. Credibility and trust are established via endorsements and success stories.

9. Engage with Trending Conversations

Engage in debates that are current and pertinent in your niche. You can increase interest in your profile by having conversations about things other than your content.

10. Personalized Engagement

Use the names of your followers wherever you can to make your discussions more relatable. It demonstrates that you regard them as unique people and not just as a digit in your following count.

Case Study: "EcoEats' Captivating Journey"

To highlight the significance of interacting with your followers, allow me to share the story of "EcoEats," a tiny food delivery service that prioritizes environmental sustainability.

Before realizing the importance of interacting with followers, "EcoEats" had trouble taking off on social media. Even though their target market consisted of foodies who were concerned about the environment, they still wanted to build a devoted following around their brand.

Here's how "EcoEats" turned things around:

Active Engagement: "EcoEats" made a concerted effort to respond to every comment on their posts, often sparking conversations about sustainability, food choices, and eco-friendly living.

User-Generated Content: They made a strong effort to get their clients to tell others about their "EcoEats" adventures. "EcoEats" highlighted instances when consumers shared images of their meals on social media by featuring the user-generated content on their profile.

Interactive Stories: "EcoEats" uses Instagram Stories to have real-time conversations with its followers. They held in-person Q&A sessions regarding their sustainable sourcing, food preparation, and environmentally friendly packaging.

Customer Stories: They frequently posted customer testimonials detailing their eco-friendly endeavors, which ranged from adopting plant-based diets to cutting down on food waste.

Educational Content: "EcoEats" published educational articles concerning how dietary decisions affect the environment. Their audience, who frequently wanted to make more environmentally friendly food choices, found value in this content.

The outcomes were astounding. "EcoEats" developed into a successful community after becoming a specialized food delivery business. Their supporters were devoted supporters of sustainable living through dietary decisions as well as customers. For their target demographic, their profile developed into a center for conversations about sustainability, green issues, and inspirational stories.

"The Engaging Journey of 'EcoEats'" is a testament to the power of engaging with followers. "EcoEats" converted followers into devoted supporters and brand ambassadors by fostering a sense of community, offering value, and engaging with their audience.

Engaging with Your Followers as a Growth Strategy

Interacting with your followers is a growth strategy in itself, not just a box to be checked. Your greatest asset is your fan base. Their involvement increases your reach, cultivates loyalty, and creates a feeling of community. You'll learn how engagement fits into your larger social media strategy as you proceed through "The Art of Social Media Growth for Small Businesses," from starting discussions to developing brand evangelists and tracking your progress. In the always-changing realm of social media, you may build a strong online community and take your small business to new heights by being an expert at communicating with your followers.

Effective Engagement Strategies

Engagement on social media is the lifeblood of your online presence. Authentic connections are made between your brand and your audience through engaging techniques that not only humanize and make it more relatable. Developing deep connections is the focus of this section,

Conversations over Broadcasting

Making the error of using social media as a broadcasting platform is among the most frequent ones. Have discussions with your audience rather than just distributing stuff. The following explains why talks are more productive:

1. Authentic Connection

Talking with customers demonstrates that there is a real person behind the brand. It encourages sincerity and increases audience trust.

2. Active Listening

Speaking and listening are equally vital in a conversation. You may learn a lot about the wants, needs, and pain points of your audience by having interactions with them.

3. Community Building

Your audience can establish a connection with one another by setting up a conversation area. It creates a sense of community and belonging around your business.

4. Instant Feedback

Discussions get instantaneous feedback. As soon as something strikes a chord with your audience, you'll know it. If something doesn't work, you can modify your plan of action.

5. Individualization

You can customize your encounters through conversations. Your audience is more inclined to interact with your brand when they feel heard and noticed.

Responding to Comments and Messages

The first step in having a discussion is to actively reply to messages and comments. It's essential to creating a vibrant community; it goes beyond simple decency. Here's how to react in a useful way:

1. Timeliness

React immediately. While you shouldn't respond to every message or comment right away, try to do so within a fair amount of time. It conveys your appreciation for their time.

2. Be Personal

Avoid generic or automated responses. Make your responses more individualized by addressing the individual's unique question or opinion and utilizing their name.

3. Acknowledge Feedback

Accept criticism in both positive and negative forms. Respond to the concerns of those who offer constructive criticism while acknowledging those who admire your brand.

4. Ask Open-Ended Questions

To spark additional discussion, think about using open-ended questions in your responses to comments. For instance, inquire about the person's experience with a comparable product if they leave a remark on a product post.

5. Handle Criticism Gracefully

It is inevitable to hear criticism or unfavorable remarks. Respond to the situation with empathy and a desire to find a solution rather than becoming defensive. This has the power to win over a disgruntled consumer's loyalty.

6. Use Humor and Emotion

Humor and emotion can be useful in answers when used appropriately. They add a human touch to your brand and improve the quality of interactions.

7. Take Conversations Private

Take the conversation to email or direct messages for more delicate or complicated concerns. This demonstrates regard for the individual's privacy.

8. Express Gratitude

We appreciate the thoughts, support, and remarks from your viewers. A small "thank you" can make a big difference in fostering positive interactions.

9. Be Consistent

Maintaining consistency in your replies is essential to developing a dependable and credible brand. Make sure that, in terms of engagement, every team member is in agreement.

10. Set Boundaries

Setting limits is just as crucial as fostering engagement. To preserve a good work-life balance, reply to messages and comments within business hours.

Case Investigation: "The Genuine Engagement of 'PetPals Paradise'"

Allow us to examine the story of "PetPals Paradise," a tiny pet-sitting service that grew into a cherished online community, in order to demonstrate the influence of successful engagement tactics.

Before understanding the significance of genuine engagement, "PetPals Paradise" faced the challenge of fierce competition in the pet-sitting industry. They had to set themselves apart and gain the confidence of pet owners.

Here's how "PetPals Paradise" achieved it:

Authentic Engagement: The owner, Emily, actively responded to comments on their posts and engaged in conversations with their audience. Emily would ask if they had any specific issues and offer useful suggestions if someone asked for pet care ideas.

User-Generated Content: Emily invited her clients to submit pictures and narratives about their animals. She honored every furry buddy on her profile, igniting discussions about animals, taking care of them, and sharing anecdotes about them.

Personalized Interactions: Emily addressed people by the name of their pets in her responses, personalizing them rather than responding in a generic manner. For example, Emily would say, "Whiskers is such a cutie!" in response to someone posting a photo of their cat. How's he doing?"

Immediate Feedback: Emily always got back to customers within an hour of them asking questions or leaving a review. In the industry, her prompt and affable reactions were noteworthy.

Expressing Gratitude: Emily frequently thanked her audience for their support and trust in "PetPals Paradise." A sense of community was nurtured by this thankfulness.

The results were remarkable. From being an ordinary pet-sitting service, "PetPals Paradise" evolved into a cherished brand with a devoted following. Their profile developed into a gathering place for pet owners to rejoice, ask for guidance, and share tales about their furry friends.

The success of genuine engagement is demonstrated by "The Genuine Engagement of 'PetPals Paradise'". "PetPals Paradise" transformed followers into devoted pet lovers that not only used their services but also praised their business by creating a community, providing value, and actually connecting with their audience.

Handling Customer Feedback and Reviews

Customer opinions and reviews have a huge impact on a brand's reputation and success in the digital era. Effectively responding to these evaluations is not only polite behavior; it's a key element of "The Art of Social Media Growth for Small Businesses." This section delves into the art of cultivating a culture of valuable feedback and handling customer reviews and feedback, both positive and negative.

Turning Negatives into Positives

Although receiving unfavorable comments or evaluations might be discouraging, they also present priceless chances for improvement. The way you respond to them can establish the essence of your brand. Here's how to make the bad into the good:

1. Respond Promptly

Respond quickly to critical comments. It demonstrates your compassion for your clients' worries and your desire to find a solution.

2. Stay Professional and Empathetic

React in an understanding and professional manner. Recognize the dissatisfaction or irritation of the client. Avoid defensive or confrontational responses.

3. Resolve Privately

Consider using a private channel, such email or direct message, for discussions involving sensitive material or in-depth discussion of the matter at hand.

4. Offer Solutions

Give a remedy or action items to deal with the issue. Demonstrate your resolve to put things right and your active efforts to find a solution.

5. Learn and Adapt

Take the time to learn from unfavorable comments. Determine the underlying reasons of the problem and make the necessary adjustments to stop it from happening again.

6. Ask for Specifics

Ask for details if the negative feedback is ambiguous so that you can better comprehend the problem. Providing more specific input can aid in identifying the issue.

7. Follow Up

Following the issue's resolution, get in touch with the client to make sure they're happy with the outcome. By going above and above, you can win over a disgruntled customer's loyalty.

8. Share Positive Outcomes

Tell your audience of the successful resolution if you were able to turn a bad situation around. This not only demonstrates your dedication to client happiness but also the responsiveness of your business.

9. Respond to All Negative Feedback

Refrain from picking and choosing which unfavorable comments to address. Consistently respond to any unfavorable evaluations and remarks.

10. Constructive Internal Feedback

Talk to your team internally about the feedback. Make use of it to pinpoint areas that need work and make adjustments to your procedures.

Encouraging Positive Feedback

Positive reviews are essential to the survival of your brand. It not only improves your reputation but also persuades prospective clients to pick up your business. Here's how to promote compliments:

1. Deliver Outstanding Service

Deliver outstanding experiences, goods, and services on a regular basis. Positive reviews are more likely to be left by clients who receive superior service.

2. Ask for Reviews

Never be afraid to request testimonials from pleased clients. Following up with a successful transaction or encounter, send follow-up emails or messages asking for evaluations and comments.

3. Create an Incentive

Take into account providing rewards for favourable reviews. This can be coupons, access to special content, or a chance to win something.

4. Streamline the Review Process

Make it simple for clients to submit reviews. Provide customers with direct links or buttons to the review platform of their choice in your emails and on your website.

5. Feature Positive Reviews

Highlight favourable comments on your website and social media accounts. This enhances your reputation and motivates other people to write evaluations.

6. Express Gratitude

We appreciate the good evaluations that customers have left. A short "thank you" expresses gratitude for their assistance and promotes more interaction.

7. Share Success Stories

Tell success stories about satisfied clients and their use of your good or service. This offers prospective customers important social proof.

8. Engage with Positive Feedback

React when you receive compliments. Thank the consumer and emphasize the good relationship you have with them.

9. Reward Loyal Customers

When rewarding loyal customers who routinely provide great reviews, think about introducing loyalty perks.

10. Consistently Deliver Value

Key is consistency. Maintain a high standard of quality and outstanding service to guarantee that favorable reviews are consistently received.

Case Investigation: "The Remarkable Turnaround of 'FreshFlavors Café'"

In order to demonstrate how to transform negative feedback into positive ones and support favorable comments, let's explore the tale of "FreshFlavors Café," a tiny eatery that is making an effort to establish itself in the cutthroat food sector.

Before understanding the significance of customer feedback, "FreshFlavors Café" faced a challenging situation. One of their customers left a bad review, saying that their food and service were not up to par.

Here's how they turned it around:

Immediate Response: "FreshFlavors Café" promised to ensure customer happiness and acknowledged the client's displeasure as soon as the negative review was placed.

Empathetic Resolution: They offered a sincere apology and suggested ways to make amends. In order to entice the customer to return and have a better eating experience, the restaurant provided them with a complementary dinner.

Internal Improvement: "FreshFlavors Café" evaluated their standards for service and food quality based on the input they received. They determined what needed to be changed and made the appropriate adjustments.

Showcase and Follow-Up: "FreshFlavors Café" checked in with the consumer to see if they were happy with their experience following their second visit. The patron wrote a glowing review, praising the restaurant for its commitment to making them feel welcome.

Reputation Boost: "FreshFlavors Café" enhanced its standing and showed its dedication to providing excellent customer service by properly handling the unfavorable review and used it to their advantage.

The story "The Remarkable Turnaround of 'FreshFlavors Café'" demonstrates the value of taking constructive criticism and using it to improve an experience. In addition to keeping a client, "FreshFlavors Café" demonstrated their drive to providing exceptional service by resolving problems with empathy and diligence.

Customer Feedback and Reviews as a Growth Strategy

Consumer opinions and evaluations are an essential component of your growth strategy, not just a byproduct of your company. Managing and promoting feedback well can convert infrequent consumers into devoted supporters. As you proceed, you will discover how to include client testimonials and reviews into a more comprehensive social media plan that covers everything from fostering success stories to assessing your progress. You can create a powerful and reliable brand and take your small business to new heights in the always-changing social media landscape by being an expert at handling reviews and comments.

Chapter five

Measuring, Analyzing, and Adapting

Key Metrics and Analytics Tools

Understanding your social media performance is essential for optimizing your approach and making informed decisions. In this chapter, "Key Metrics and Analytics Tools: Tracking What Matters, Google Analytics, Social Insights, and More," we delve into the world of metrics and analytics tools and how they can supercharge your journey.

Tracking What Matters

Posting content and hoping for the best isn't enough to make your social media strategy effective. It all comes down to knowing how well your content is performing, what your audience is responding to, and where you can make improvements. The following crucial metrics are important:

1. Follower Growth Rate

This metric indicates how quickly your follower base is growing. Monitoring is crucial since a consistently increasing number of followers may be a sign of a strong social media presence.

2. Engagement Rate

Likes, comments, shares, and clicks on your content are all considered forms of engagement. A high amount of engagement indicates that your audience is connecting with your material.

3. Click-Through Rate (CTR)

CTR counts the frequency with which readers click on links or calls to action within your posts. It's essential for determining how well your content performs and for increasing visitors to your website or landing pages.

4. Conversion Rate

The percentage of users who interact with your social media content and then complete a desired action, such as making a purchase, is tracked by your conversion rate.

5. Bounce Rate

In case you are driving visitors to your website, the bounce rate matters. It calculates the proportion of site visitors that depart without taking any further action.

6. Post Reach

The number of unique users that have viewed your content is shown by post reach. It is necessary to comprehend the visibility of your material.

7. Return on Investment (ROI)

By comparing the revenue from your social media efforts to your total costs, ROI helps you assess the performance of your social media strategy.

8. Customer Lifetime Value (CLV)

CLV determines a customer's long-term worth. Gaining an understanding of this measure will enable you to customize your social media approach to draw in and keep valuable clients.

9. Social Share of Voice (SOV)

SOV calculates your brand's percentage of the total social media discourse within your industry or niche. It aids in your comprehension of the position of your brand about rivals.

10. Audience Demographics

It's essential to comprehend the age, gender, geography, and other demographics of your audience to customize your targeting and content.

Google Analytics, Social Insights, and More

Google Analytics is an effective tool for monitoring your website's performance, including the traffic it receives from social media posts. Here's how to make good use of it:

Website Traffic: Google Analytics gives you a thorough understanding of the amount of visitors to your website. You can see the social media sites bringing in the most traffic, the content your visitors are engaging with, and the routes they take across your website.

Conversion Tracking: Using Google Analytics, you can create conversion goals to monitor actions influenced by your social media efforts, such as downloads, sign-ups, and purchases.

Audience Insights: Google Analytics offers demographic and interest data about your website visitors, helping you understand the characteristics of your audience.

Behavior Flow: This feature lets you see how visitors navigate your website by displaying where they come in, what pages they view, and where they go out.

Acquisition Reports: These reports let you examine how well each social media network drives visitors and conversions by breaking down traffic sources in depth.

Social Insights: Every social media network offers a unique collection of analytics and insights tools. These are some of the most important things you may learn from well-known platforms.

Understanding your social media performance is essential for optimizing your approach and making informed decisions. In this chapter, "Key Metrics and Analytics Tools: Tracking What Matters, Google Analytics, Social Insights, and More," we delve into the world of metrics and analytics tools and how they can supercharge your journey.

Interpreting Data to Improve Strategy

Data is a wealth of knowledge that may show you the way to success in the social media industry. It takes more than merely gathering data to evaluate it, turn findings into workable strategies, and implement them. We go into the art of data interpretation and its crucial function.

Making Data-Driven Decisions

Making decisions based on empirical evidence, statistics, and analytics is known as data-driven decision-making. It is a crucial part of a successful social media plan. Here's how to decide based on data:

1. Set Clear Objectives

Make sure you know exactly what your goals are for social media before you start. Your aims will determine what information you need to gather, whether it's for improving sales, expanding brand awareness, or growing website traffic.

2. Define Key Performance Indicators (KPIs)

The precise measurements that support your goals are known as KPIs. KPIs could include the amount of unique visitors to your website or click-through rates (CTR) if your objective is to increase website traffic.

3. Collect Relevant Data

To collect information on the KPIs you have selected, use analytics tools. These tools offer insights into your audience engagement, social media performance, and other areas.

4. Analyze and Interpret Data

Analyzing and interpreting the data is the next stage after gathering it. Finding correlations, trends, and patterns in the data is necessary for this.

5. Derive Insights

Insights are the valuable conclusions drawn from data analysis. They assist you in determining what is effective, ineffective, and areas in need of improvement.

6. Identify Areas for Improvement

Determine which aspects of your social media approach require improvement in light of the insights. Content, publishing schedules, audience targeting, and engagement strategies are a few examples of this.

7. Test and Iterate

Make adjustments in light of your data-driven findings. Continuous improvement is a crucial component of data-driven decision-making. Evaluate novel tactics, gauge their results, and make necessary adjustments.

8. Monitor Progress

Keep an eye on your data often to see how your adjustments are impacting it. Monitoring your data guarantees that your efforts are directed appropriately.

Adjusting Your Approach Based on Insights

Interpreting data involves more than just analysis; it also involves acting on the knowledge you have obtained. Here's how to modify your strategy in light of data insights:

1. Content Strategy

Make necessary adjustments to your content strategy if data analysis shows that some content performs better than others. Make more of the content that appeals to your audience your main priority.

2. Posting Schedule Analyze when your audience is most active and engaged. For optimal visibility and interaction, modify your posting schedule to coincide with these peak periods.

3. Audience Targeting

Refine your audience targeting to reach the proper people if insights show that the demographics or interests of your audience differ from what you had previously anticipated.

4. Engagement Tactics

If certain engagement tactics, such as asking questions or running polls, are more effective in driving interactions, incorporate them into your strategy.

5. Ad Spend Allocation

Data insights might help you allocate your advertising budget. Reallocate your spending if you discover that a particular platform or campaign is yielding a better return on investment.

6. Conversion Optimization

In order to raise the conversion rate, focus on streamlining the step of the conversion funnel where your data indicates a bottleneck.

7. A/B Testing

Conduct A/B testing to try several strategies and identify the most effective one. Your strategy can be improved with A/B testing if you base your decisions on data.

8. Social Media Platform Selection

Consider allocating more of your money and efforts to the platform that performs best if you find that it routinely outperforms the others.

The case "The Adaptive Success of 'Artistic Expressions'" is examined.

Let's examine the tale of "Artistic Expressions," a tiny online art gallery that aimed to increase its social media presence, to highlight the value of data-driven decision-making and the adaptation of plans based on findings.

Before adopting data-driven decision-making, "Artistic Expressions" encountered difficulties growing its web presence. They were having trouble drawing in a loyal following on social media and were getting little interaction from their posts.

Here's how they turned things around:

Data Collection: "Artistic Expressions" began tracking the effectiveness of their social media posts. They monitored indicators such as click-through rates, post reach, and engagement rates.

Data Analysis: They found that posts containing artist interviews and behind-the-scenes content had substantially greater engagement rates. They changed their content approach as a result of this data-driven understanding.

Content Strategy Adjustment: "Artistic Expressions" shifted their content focus to include more behind-the-scenes content, artist spotlights, and in-depth interviews. Their audience responded favorably to these modifications, which raised participation.

A/B Testing: They tested post formats, images, and posting times in order to further hone their content strategy. They determined the best posting schedule and content type for optimum interaction through these testing.

Platform Allocation: Their most engaged platform was Instagram, according to data insights. "Artistic Expressions" made the decision to scale back on less successful platforms and devote more time and resources to Instagram.

Refinement of Audience Targeting: Based on insights, art enthusiasts and collectors made up the majority of their audience. In order to more successfully reach this segment, they modified their audience targeting.

Conversion Funnel Optimization: When users tried to make purchases, the statistics indicated a bottleneck in the conversion funnel. "Artistic Expressions" improved the purchasing process by streamlining it, which increased conversion rates.

The results were remarkable. "Artistic Expressions" considerably boosted their internet presence and art sales by employing data-driven decision-making and adapting their strategy in response to insights.

"The Adaptive Success of 'Artistic Expressions'" showcases the power of data interpretation and the adjustment of strategies based on insights. Businesses can optimize their social media strategies and achieve significant growth by adopting data-driven decision-making.

Interpreting Data to Improve Strategy as a Growth Strategy

Analyzing data to enhance strategy is a continuous activity rather than a one-time event. Through data-driven decision-making and insight-driven approach adjustments, you may optimize your social media strategy to attain impressive growth. As you proceed, you'll discover how to include data interpretation into your whole social media strategy, from targeting and content optimization to ROI measurement and approach optimization. Gaining proficiency in data-driven decision-making will enable you to modify and advance your approach in the dynamic realm of social media.

Adapting to Algorithm Changes

The social media landscape is always changing, and algorithms are a major factor in deciding how visible and successful your content is. You have to remain ahead of algorithm changes and modify your approach as necessary if you want to succeed in this fast-paced environment. This session delves into the skill of navigating social media algorithms and making sure your small business keeps expanding.

The Ever-Evolving Social Media Landscape

Social media systems are dynamic, ever-changing to satisfy user demands and accommodate new trends. Algorithms, the intricate formulas that decide what information shows in a user's feed, have undergone adjustments as part of this progression. Here are some explanations for why the social media scene is constantly evolving:

1. User Behavior

As user behavior shifts, social media platforms need to adjust their algorithms to ensure users see content that is relevant and engaging. For instance, algorithm priorities have changed as a result of the popularity of stories and video content on social media sites like Instagram.

2. Platform Growth

Social media companies' algorithms must change as they expand and become more diverse in order to meet the needs of the market, user demographics, and new forms of content.

3. Monetization Strategies

A lot of social networking sites make money from advertisements. Algorithm priority changes may incentivize companies to increase their advertising spending, which may have an effect on organic reach.

4. Competitive Landscape

There is intense rivalry for attention as more businesses and individuals use social media. Changing algorithms aims to maintain user engagement and balance the visibility of material.

Staying Ahead of Algorithm Updates

Sustaining your social media presence and growing requires you to adjust to algorithm changes. Here's how to keep up with algorithm changes:

1. Stay Informed

Keep an eye on the news and updates on social media from the sites you frequent. Platforms frequently publish updates outlining algorithm modifications and their effects.

2. Analyze Data

Examine your data on a regular basis to see how changes in the algorithm impact the performance of your content.

Keep an eye on indicators such as click-through rates, engagement, and reach.

3. Test and Experiment

Try a variety of publishing techniques and content kinds to see what works best. You can determine what functions best in the current algorithmic environment with the use of A/B testing.

4. Diversify Content

Create a broad spectrum of content that is in line with the current priorities of the platform. For instance, think about include more videos in your plan if a platform prioritizes video content.

5. Engage with Your Audience

By actively interacting with your audience—that is, by answering messages and comments—you may tell algorithms that your content is worthwhile and worthy of being seen.

6. Stay Authentic

Avoid shortcuts or black-hat techniques to game the system. Algorithms are made to recognize and penalize behavior that is not legitimate.

7. Leverage Ads

To increase the visibility of your content, think about utilizing sponsored advertising. Paid content is frequently given priority in consumers' feeds on social media networks.

8. Collaborate and Network

Take part in networking and cooperation within your sector. The reach and engagement of your work can be increased by collaborating with others.

9. Join Communities

Engage in social media groups and communities related to your niche. Participating actively in these forums can increase the visibility of your material.

10. Adapt Your Posting Schedule Adjust your posting schedule to align with peak activity times on the platform. This can improve the likelihood that people will see your article.

Case Study Analysis: "TechGear Innovations' Adaptive Success"

Let's examine the tale of "TechGear Innovations," a tiny technology review blog that mostly relied on its social media presence to reach its audience, to highlight the importance of staying ahead of algorithm modifications.

Prior to fully realizing the effects of algorithm modifications, "TechGear Innovations" encountered difficulties keeping their social media material visible and engaging.

Here's how they adapted:

Algorithm Monitoring: The "TechGear Innovations" crew kept a careful eye on announcements and updates from the social media sites they visited. They also signed up for blogs and newsletters that provided social media updates.

Data Analysis: They conducted a thorough analysis of the reach, engagement, and most successful post kinds for their social media material.

Content Diversification: They added video reviews to their written pieces in order to diversify their material, realizing that algorithms were favoring video content more than textual information.

Experimentation: The team experimented with posting times and strategies to discover when their audience was most active and engaged. To improve their posting strategies, they conducted A/B testing.

Collaborations: They requested cooperation and shout-outs from other tech bloggers and influencers. Their content became more visible as a result of these partnerships.

Paid Advertising: By designating a portion of their budget for paid advertising, "TechGear Innovations" was able to increase the visibility of their most significant reviews and guides.

Engagement: By quickly answering questions and leaving comments, they demonstrated active audience engagement. This improved the likelihood that algorithms will find their information valuable.

The results were impressive. "TechGear Innovations" maintained their social media presence and reached a larger audience by modifying their approach in response to algorithm updates.

A case study titled "The Adaptive Success of 'TechGear Innovations'" emphasizes how important it is to plan ahead for algorithm updates and adjust your approach to deal with the ever-evolving social media ecosystem.

Adapting to Algorithm Changes as a Growth Strategy

Being ahead of algorithm adjustments is not only a recommended practice, but also a survival strategy in the dynamic world of social media. You can continue to expand your small business and negotiate the always changing social media world by remaining informed, evaluating data, trying new things, and adjusting.

Conclusion

Your Path to Social Media Success

Congratulations on completing "The Art of Social Media Growth for Small Businesses." Your journey through this book has equipped you with the knowledge and strategies necessary to harness the power of social media to grow your small business. As we conclude, let's take a moment to celebrate your achievements and understand that social media success is an ongoing journey.

Celebrating Your Achievements

Throughout this journey, you've gained valuable insights and tools to make your social media endeavors a resounding success. You've learned how to:

Craft an Engaging Content Strategy: Developing a content strategy that resonates with your audience and keeps them coming back for more.

Master the Art of Storytelling on Social Media: Building a connection with your audience by weaving compelling narratives that capture the essence of your brand.

Harness the Power of Visual Content: Understanding the impact of images and videos and using design tips and tools to create captivating visuals.

Grow Your Follower Base: Implementing strategies for organic growth and engaging with your followers to foster a loyal community.

Employ Effective Engagement Strategies: Prioritizing conversations over broadcasting and responding to comments and messages to build trust and relationships.

Handle Customer Feedback and Reviews: Transforming negatives into positives and encouraging positive feedback to strengthen your brand's reputation.

Utilize Key Metrics and Analytics Tools: Tracking what matters and making data-driven decisions to refine your social media strategy.

Interpret Data to Improve Strategy: Continually analyzing data and making informed adjustments to stay relevant in the ever-evolving social media landscape.

Adapt to Algorithm Changes: Navigating the dynamic world of social media by staying ahead of algorithm updates and adjusting your approach accordingly.

These achievements are milestones on your path to social media success. It's essential to recognize your dedication and progress as you continue your journey.

The Ongoing Journey of Social Media Growth

Social media success is not a destination; it's a journey that requires ongoing dedication and adaptation. As the social media landscape evolves and user behaviors change, you must remain flexible and receptive to new strategies and insights.

Here are some key takeaways to remember as you continue your journey:

Stay Informed: The social media landscape is constantly changing. Keep yourself updated on platform changes, trends, and emerging technologies to adapt your strategy accordingly.

Experiment and Test: Don't be afraid to try new approaches and conduct A/B testing. These experiments can reveal what works best for your unique audience.

Engage Authentically: Authentic engagement with your audience is the bedrock of social media success. Respond to comments, messages, and feedback with sincerity and empathy.

Monitor Your Data: Regularly analyze your social media metrics to track your progress and make data-driven decisions for continuous improvement.

Embrace Challenges: Challenges are opportunities in disguise. When faced with obstacles, view them as chances to learn, adapt, and grow.

Collaborate and Network: Building relationships with others in your industry can extend your reach and open doors to new opportunities for growth.

Celebrate Successes: Acknowledge your milestones and achievements. These celebrations can fuel your motivation and drive for continued growth.

Remember, the journey of social media growth is unique to your small business. It's not about competing with others but about reaching your specific goals and creating a thriving online presence that serves your audience.

As you continue on your path to social media success, keep the knowledge and strategies from this book close at hand. Whether you're crafting engaging content, interpreting data, or adapting to algorithm changes, these tools will be your allies in the dynamic world of social media.

Thank you for embarking on this journey with "The Art of Social Media Growth for Small Businesses." Your small business has the potential to achieve remarkable success in the ever-evolving world of social media. May your continued efforts and dedication lead to the growth and prosperity you deserve. Cheers to your social media success!

:

: